Could you live in a house made of snow?

Igloo

the BIG PICTURE

Louise Spilsbury

Published 2010 by
A&C Black Publishers Ltd.
36 Soho Square, London, W1D 3QY

www.acblack.com

ISBN HB 978-1-4081-2791-9
      PB 978-1-4081-3157-2

Text copyright © 2010 Louise Spilsbury

This book is produced using paper that is made from wood grown in managed, sustainable forests. It is natural, renewable and recyclable. The logging and manufacturing processes conform to the environmental regulations of the country of origin.

Produced for A&C Black by Calcium. www.calciumcreative.co.uk

Printed and bound in China by C&C Offset Printing Co.

All the internet addresses given in this book were correct at the time of going to press. The author and publishers regret any inconvenience caused if addresses have changed or sites have ceased to exist, but can accept no responsibility for any such changes.

Acknowledgements

The publishers would like to thank the following for their kind permission to reproduce their photographs:

Cover: Photolibrary: Radius Images (front), Shutterstock: Geoffrey Kuchera (back). **Pages:** Alamy Images: Picture Contact/Ton Koene 20; Corbis: Wolfgang Kaehler 10; Fotolia: AlexQ 19, Michael Kempf 12-13, Tyler Olson 6-7; Istockphoto: Michael Olson 4-5; Photolibrary: White Fox 9, 14-15; Rex Features: Martha Holmes/Nature Picture Library 6-7; Shutterstock: Eyespeak 3, Geoffrey Kuchera 17, Laila R 4-5, 14-15, Tropinina Olga 12-13, Tyler Olson 1, 2-3, 8-9, 10-11, 16-17, 18-19, 20-21, 22-23, 24.

Contents

Igloos 4

Build it Up 6

Look Inside 8

Keep Warm 10

Igloo Food....................... 12

On a Hunt 14

In the Sun 16

Getting Around 18

Today................................ 20

Glossary 22

Further Reading 23

Index 24

Igloos

Igloos are amazing houses built from just snow and ice. People called Inuits **used to live in igloos.**

Igloos today

Most Inuits do not live in igloos anymore. Today, igloos are mainly built for fun.

Snow place like home!

Warm inside

Igloos are built in places that are covered with snow and ice. But inside the igloo it can be warm and cosy.

Igloos are strong. A man could stand on top of one without crushing it.

5

Build it Up

People can make an igloo anywhere there is snow that is hard enough to walk on.

Round and round

First, people cut thick blocks of snow. They put them in a circle. Then they put more blocks on top to build up the igloo.

Igloos are built with thick, strong blocks of snow.

Keep out cold

When the igloo is built, people cover it with snow to stop the wind and rain getting inside.

Block by block

Look Inside

In the past, Inuits kept warm inside their igloos for most of the winter.

Light and heat

To light up the igloo, Inuits made candles from **seal blubber**. The candles also helped to keep out the cold.

Warm and cosy

Bedtime

At night, Inuits slept in sleeping bags.
They were made from **reindeer** skins.
The fur on the inside was warm and soft.

You can even have a fire inside an igloo.

9

Keep Warm

Igloos are cosy, but people still need to wear thick clothes to keep warm inside them.

Making clothes

Inuits made clothes from the skins of animals, such as bears and deer.

Inuits called their furry jackets parkas.

Tough boots

Inuits made boots from seal skin. The skin is **waterproof**, so the boots kept out wet snow and ice.

I'm warm

Igloo Food

In places where people build igloos, it is too cold for many plants to grow. People who live here mainly eat meat.

Eat up

Inuits ate animals such as fish, whales, **walruses**, and seals. They ate their meat **raw**.

Inuits hunted walruses for their meat.

Keep it fresh

Inuits stored meat and fish by burying it in the ice. Then they covered it with rocks to stop animals from digging it up.

Freezing cold

In the Sun

**When summer comes, the sun
and warm weather melt igloos.**

Summer living

In summer, Inuits lived in a tent.
The tent was made of seal or
reindeer skins stretched
over a wooden frame.

It's melting

Busy days

Inuits used the summer to collect food such as wild berries. They stored them to eat in winter.

Reindeer skin was used for summer tents.

17

Getting Around

Inuits used dogs and sleds to travel in the past. Today, they use high speed sleds to cross the snow.

Super sleds

Modern Inuit sleds are very fast and powerful. They are powered by a motor.

The sleds Inuits use today are called skidoos.

Zoom!

Tough dogs

Inuit sleds were pulled by husky dogs in the past. These are big dogs that are able to survive in very cold places.

Today

Most Inuits now live in modern, heated houses. They can also buy their food from shops.

Remembering

Winters are long and cold where Inuit people live. To pass the time, they sometimes tell stories about what Inuit life was like in the past.

Life for young Inuits today is very different from the past.

Igloos today

Although most Inuits now live in modern houses, some Inuits still build igloos when they go on hunting trips.

Glossary

blubber thick fat from the body of an animal

Inuits people who live in northern Canada, Greenland, and the Arctic

raw not cooked

reindeer animal with long horns on its head. Reindeers live in cold places.

seal animal with flippers that lives on the land and in the water

sleds vehicles used to travel across snow

walruses animals with flippers and sharp tusks. Walruses live on land and in the water in very cold places.

waterproof keeps out water

Further Reading

Websites

Watch how the entrance to an igloo is made at:
www.people.howstuffworks.com/igloo.htm

Find out more about Inuits and igloos at:
www.windows.ucar.edu/tour/link=/earth/polar/ inuit_image_gallery.html

Books

Living in the Arctic (Rookie Read-About Geography) by Allan Fowler, Children's Press (2001).

Arctic and Antarctic (DK Eye Wonder), by Lorrie Mack, Dorling Kindersley (2006).

The Inuit Thought of It: Amazing Arctic Innovations (We Thought of It) by Alootook Ipellie and David MacDonald, Annick Press (2007).

Index

burying 13

candles 8
clothes 10

fire 8
fish 12, 13, 14
fishing 14
food 12–13, 17, 20

houses 20, 21
hunting 12, 14–15
husky dogs 19

ice 4, 5, 11, 13, 14
Inuits 4

kayaks 15

meat 12, 13

parkas 10

raw meat 12
reindeer skin 9, 16, 17

seal blubber 8
seal skin 11, 16
skidoos 18
skins 9, 10, 11, 16, 17
sleds 18–19
sleeping bags 9
snow blocks 6, 7
strong 5

walruses 12
waterproof 11

24